THE BEST NFL
QUARTERBACKS
OF ALL TIME

By Matt Scheff

Published by ABDO Publishing Company, PO Box 398166, Minneapolis, MN 55439. Copyright © 2014 by Abdo Consulting Group, Inc. International copyrights reserved in all countries. No part of this book may be reproduced in any form without written permission from the publisher. SportsZone™ is a trademark and logo of ABDO Publishing Company.

Printed in the United States of America,
North Mankato, Minnesota
052013
112013
♻ THIS BOOK CONTAINS AT LEAST 10% RECYCLED MATERIALS.

Editor: Chrös McDougall
Series Designer: Christa Schneider

Photo Credits: AL Golub/AP Images, cover (left), 1 (left), 29; Tom DiPace/AP Images, cover (right), 1 (right), 33, 39, 41; NFL Photos/Vic Stein/ AP Images, 7; AP Images, 9, 27; NFL Photos/AP Images, 11, 13, 15, 19, 21, 23, 25, 43; Bettmann/Corbis/AP Images, 17; Paul Spinelli/ AP Images, 31; Mike Eliason/AP Images, 35; Rob Brown/NFL Photos/AP Images, 37; David Scarbrough/AP Images, 45; David Stluka/AP Images, 47; Jim Slosiarek/Racine Journal Times/AP Images, 49; Scott Boehm/ AP Images, 51, 59; Darron Cummings/AP Images, 53; Evan Pinkus/AP Images, 55; David J. Phillip/AP Images, 57; G. Newman Lowrance/AP Images, 61

Library of Congress Control Number: 2013931963

Cataloging-in-Publication Data
Scheff, Matt.
 The best NFL quarterbacks of all time / Matt Scheff.
   p. cm. -- (NFL's best ever)
Includes bibliographical references and index.
ISBN 978-1-61783-910-8
1. National Football League--Juvenile literature. 2. Quarterbacking (Football)--Juvenile literature. 3. Quarterbacks (Football)--Juvenile literature. I. Title.
796.332--dc23

                                                    2013931963

TABLE OF CONTENTS

INTRODUCTION

Few positions in team sports are more important than quarterback.

A quarterback touches the ball on every play. Fans give him much of the credit when his team wins—and the blame when it loses. The National Football League (NFL) has seen dozens of amazingly talented passers. They are the ones with the golden arms. They are the ones who could beat you with a run as easily as a pass. They are the ones who studied the game and understood it inside and out. But the truly great quarterbacks are at their best when the game is on the line.

Here are some of the best quarterbacks in NFL history.

OTTO GRAHAM

The 1950 NFL title was on the line.
The Cleveland Browns had the ball with less than two minutes to play. They were behind the Los Angeles Rams by one point. Browns quarterback Otto Graham led the charge. He ran the ball for 14 yards. Then he completed three big passes. Graham ran it one more time to set up the game-winning field goal. The Browns were the NFL champs in their first year in the league.

Graham was an amazing athlete. He also played pro basketball. Fans called him "Automatic Otto" because of his accurate arm. But that wasn't his only weapon. Graham also could run like a running back. The combination made him almost unstoppable. And if that wasn't enough, he also was a standout defensive back.

Otto Graham of the Cleveland Browns was one of the NFL's first star quarterbacks.

Graham started with the Browns in 1946. At the time, Cleveland played in the All-America Football Conference (AAFC). The AAFC was a pro league that tried to compete with the NFL. The league lasted just four years. Graham led the Browns to all four of those championships.

Then in 1950, the Browns joined the NFL and claimed the NFL title (the Super Bowl did not begin until after the 1966 season).

Graham played a total of 10 pro seasons. He led the Browns to the league championship game in every one of them. In his six seasons in the NFL, he led the league in completion percentage three times. He also won three Most Valuable Player (MVP) Awards. But perhaps what people remember most about Graham was that he was the ultimate winner. No other quarterback has ever had such an amazing run of success.

10

The number of league championship games to which Graham led his team, one for every year he played professionally.

Otto Graham spins around a tackler for a Cleveland Browns touchdown in 1954.

OTTO GRAHAM

Hometown: Waukegan, Illinois

College: Northwestern University

Height, Weight: 6-foot-1, 196 pounds

Birth Date: December 6, 1921

Team: Cleveland Browns (1946–55)

All-Pro: 1947, 1948, 1949, 1951, 1953, 1954, 1955

Pro Bowls: 1950, 1951, 1952, 1953, 1954

JOHNNY UNITAS

Johnny Unitas earned his nickname, "Mr. Clutch," in the 1958 NFL title game.

Unitas and his Baltimore Colts trailed the New York Giants 17–14. Around two minutes remained. Unitas completed seven straight passes to set up a field goal to tie the game. Then in overtime, he led the Colts on the game-winning drive. Many football fans refer to this game as "The Greatest Game Ever Played."

Unitas was a one-of-a-kind player. He was a ninth-round draft choice of the Pittsburgh Steelers in 1955. The Steelers cut him. But Unitas refused to give up. He played semipro football for just $6 a game. Then the Colts saw him and signed him as a backup.

Johnny Unitas drops back during a Baltimore Colts game against the New York Jets in 1970.

Unitas got a chance to play in his fourth game with the Colts. His first pass was intercepted. But Unitas bounced back. He eventually claimed the starting job and went on to become perhaps the finest passer ever to play the game.

Unitas led the Colts to the NFL title in 1958 and 1959. He also helped them win Super Bowl V after the 1970 season. Unitas was a three-time MVP (1959, 1964, and 1967) and a 10-time Pro Bowl selection. When he retired, his 40,239 career passing yards and 290 career passing touchdowns were league records.

Unitas played during an era of football where few rules protected quarterbacks and receivers. Yet even through 2012, he remained fourteenth all-time in passing yards and ninth all-time in passing touchdowns. Fans can only imagine what kind of stats he might have racked up in today's pass-friendly league.

47

The number of consecutive games in which Unitas threw at least one touchdown pass, from 1956 to 1960. That record stood until 2012.

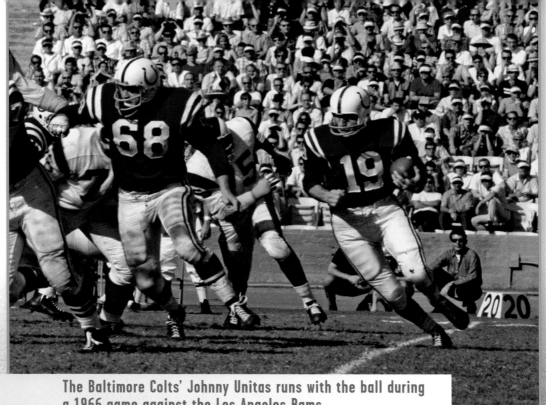

The Baltimore Colts' Johnny Unitas runs with the ball during a 1966 game against the Los Angeles Rams.

JOHNNY UNITAS

Hometown: Pittsburgh, Pennsylvania

College: University of Louisville

Height, Weight: 6-foot-1, 194 pounds

Birth Date: May 7, 1933

Teams: Baltimore Colts (1956–72)
San Diego Chargers (1973)

All-Pro: 1958, 1959, 1964, 1965, 1967

Pro Bowls: 1957, 1958, 1959, 1960, 1961, 1962, 1963, 1964, 1966, 1967

Super Bowls: III, V

BART STARR

It was a bitterly cold day at the 1967 NFL Championship Game. The Dallas Cowboys led the Green Bay Packers 17–14.

That's when quarterback Bart Starr led the Packers down the field. With 16 seconds left, the Packers were at the 1-yard line.

Starr lined up behind center. When he took the snap, he watched two Packers linemen flatten a Cowboys defender. The middle of the field was open. So Starr took off. He crashed through the hole for a touchdown. The Packers won the famous "Ice Bowl" and went on to the second Super Bowl.

Bart Starr led the Green Bay Packers' dynasty of the 1960s.

Starr's leadership and accurate arm helped the Packers build a dynasty in the 1960s. Starr wasn't the fastest quarterback. He didn't have the strongest arm. But he did have an amazing ability to see the field and make the right decision. Starr didn't need to throw 80-yard bombs. He was content to carve up a defense a few yards at a time.

Starr almost missed the chance to be great. He was a seventeenth-round draft choice in 1956. And he barely played in his first three years. But then he got his opportunity and he didn't let it go. The Packers lost in Starr's first playoff game as a starter. But Starr never lost another one after that. He led the NFL in passing yards three times. He was the 1966 league MVP. And he also was named the MVP of each of the first two Super Bowls—not bad for a seventeenth-round draft pick.

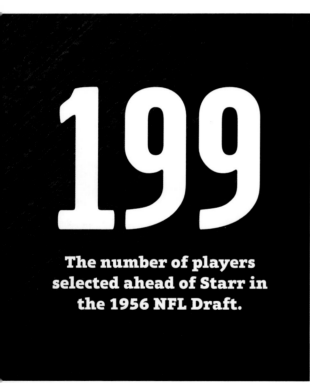

199

The number of players selected ahead of Starr in the 1956 NFL Draft.

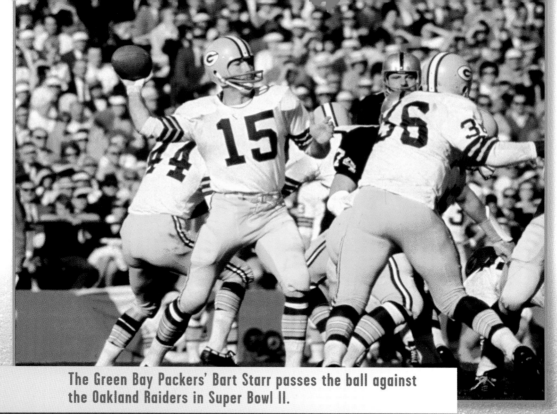

The Green Bay Packers' Bart Starr passes the ball against the Oakland Raiders in Super Bowl II.

BART STARR

Hometown: Montgomery, Alabama
College: University of Alabama
Height, Weight: 6-foot-1, 197 pounds
Birth Date: January 9, 1934
Team: Green Bay Packers (1956–71)
All-Pro: 1966
Pro Bowls: 1960, 1961, 1962, 1966
Super Bowls: I, II

ROGER STAUBACH

Only seconds remained in the game.
The Dallas Cowboys had the ball at midfield. The Minnesota Vikings led 14–10. Dallas quarterback Roger Staubach stood in the shotgun formation and took the snap. Wide receiver Drew Pearson streaked down the field. Staubach did a pump fake. Then he rifled the ball toward Pearson. The defender fell down, and Pearson caught the pass for a touchdown. Staubach called the play a "Hail Mary," which is a Roman Catholic prayer. Ever since, any long, desperate pass has gone by the same name.

Staubach was the ultimate big-game quarterback. Fans called him "Captain Comeback" for his ability to make big plays and bring his team back from behind. And his great scrambling ability earned him the nickname "Roger the Dodger."

Roger Staubach led the great Dallas Cowboys teams of the 1970s.

"Roger Staubach might be the best combination of a passer, an athlete, and a leader ever to play in the NFL," Dallas coach Tom Landry said.

Staubach got a late start in the NFL. He served in the Vietnam War until age 27. Finally in 1971 he got the job as the Cowboys' starter at age 29. He never looked back. Staubach led Dallas to a Super Bowl title that season and was the game's MVP. During his eight years as a starter, Staubach and his Cowboys played in six conference title games. He also played in four Super Bowls, winning two of them. The Cowboys also reached a Super Bowl before Staubach was the starter. Many Dallas fans consider him to be the greatest player in Cowboys history.

23

The number of game-winning drives Staubach led, 14 of which were comebacks.

Roger Staubach stands behind his Dallas Cowboys offensive line and calls out signals during a 1978 game.

ROGER STAUBACH

Hometown: Cincinnati, Ohio

College: US Naval Academy

Height, Weight: 6-foot-3, 197 pounds

Birth Date: February 5, 1942

Team: Dallas Cowboys (1969–79)

Pro Bowls: 1971, 1975, 1976, 1977, 1978, 1979

Super Bowls: V, VI, X, XII, XIII

TERRY BRADSHAW

The Pittsburgh Steelers were clinging to a three-point lead in Super Bowl IX.
Quarterback Terry Bradshaw took the field against the powerful Minnesota Vikings' defense. He led a long drive, completing pass after pass. Finally, he zipped one into the end zone. Tight end Larry Brown hauled it in for a touchdown. The Steelers had won the game. It was their first championship since debuting in 1933.

Bradshaw was a pure winner. He used his rocket arm to lead the Steelers to the playoffs year after year. He also was a clutch player. He always seemed to play his best during the postseason. He and the Steelers won an amazing four Super Bowls in six years. In those four championship games, Bradshaw threw nine touchdown passes.

Terry Bradshaw provided the offensive spark for the dominant Pittsburgh Steelers in the 1970s.

Bradshaw wasn't an instant star, though. He struggled after joining the Steelers in 1970. His coach even benched him for several games in 1974. But when Bradshaw earned back his job, he was better than ever. He and the Steelers went on to become one of the greatest NFL dynasties of all time.

Bradshaw's best year was 1978. He led the NFL with 28 touchdown passes. He was named both league MVP and Super Bowl MVP. Then he won another Super Bowl MVP title the next year. Bradshaw's statistics aren't as good as some of the other top quarterbacks of all time. But few of them had more success when it mattered most.

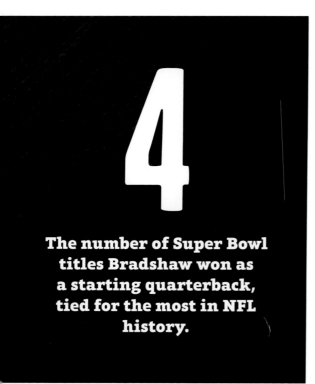

4

The number of Super Bowl titles Bradshaw won as a starting quarterback, tied for the most in NFL history.

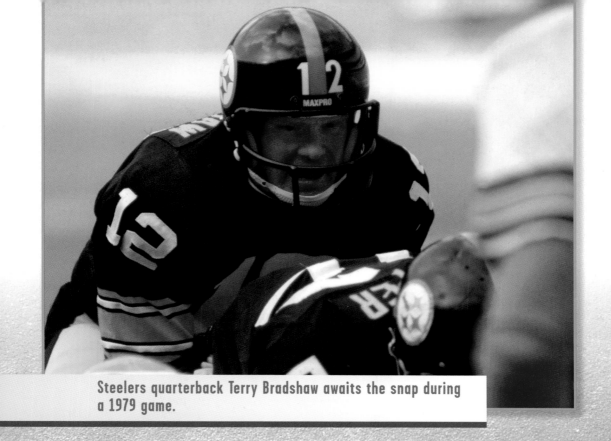

Steelers quarterback Terry Bradshaw awaits the snap during a 1979 game.

TERRY BRADSHAW

Hometown: Shreveport, Louisiana

College: Louisiana Tech University

Height, Weight: 6-foot-3, 215 pounds

Birth Date: September 2, 1948

Team: Pittsburgh Steelers (1970–83)

All-Pro: 1978

Pro Bowls: 1975, 1978, 1979

Super Bowls: IX, X, XIII, XIV

JOE MONTANA

The play that began Joe Montana's brilliant run at the top of the NFL became known simply as "The Catch."
It was the conference championship game after the 1981 season. Montana's San Francisco 49ers were down 27–21 to the Dallas Cowboys. He had just led his team on an amazing drive. With pass after pass, Montana had driven the 49ers from their own 11-yard line to the Dallas 6-yard line. But time was running out.

Montana took the snap. His primary receiver was covered. But then he saw Dwight Clark streaking across the field. So Montana threw the ball in his direction. The pass was high. But Clark reached out and snatched it out of the air for a touchdown. The 49ers won the game, and the legend of Joe Montana began.

Joe Montana led the San Francisco 49ers' West Coast offense to four Super Bowls.

Many quarterbacks of his time relied on strong arms and long passes. But the 49ers' West Coast offense focused on short, safe passes. And Montana was the perfect quarterback for that style. He was accurate and smart. He never seemed to let the pressure get to him. His teammates called him "Joe Cool" because he was always so calm.

"With all the . . . pressure, Joe has always appeared to be passive," 49ers coach Bill Walsh said. "But under the surface there was this tremendous energy, this magnetic ability to rise to the occasion."

Montana and the 49ers built a dynasty in the 1980s. They won four Super Bowls.

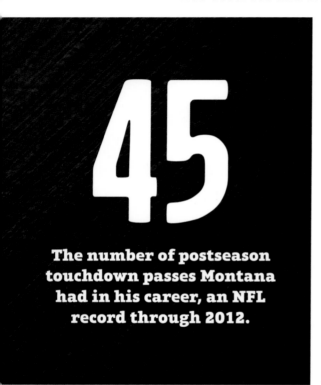

45

The number of postseason touchdown passes Montana had in his career, an NFL record through 2012.

Montana was the MVP in three of them. He also led the league in completion percentage five times. Plus Montana was the 1989 and 1990 NFL MVP. When it comes to great quarterbacks, it is hard to top Montana.

The San Francisco 49ers' Joe Montana releases a pass during a 1988 game against the Washington Redskins.

JOE MONTANA

Hometown: Monongahela, Pennsylvania

College: University of Notre Dame

Height, Weight: 6-foot-2, 200 pounds

Birth Date: June 11, 1956

Teams: San Francisco 49ers (1979–92)
Kansas City Chiefs (1993–94)

All-Pro: 1987, 1989, 1990

Pro Bowls: 1981, 1983, 1984, 1985, 1987, 1989, 1990, 1993

Super Bowls: XVI, XIX, XXIII, XXIV

DAN MARINO

Dan Marino stood in the pocket in the 1984 conference title game. The Pittsburgh Steelers' defense could not figure out how to stop him. When they brought pressure, Marino used his famous quick release to get the ball to an open receiver. When Pittsburgh played back, Marino stood calmly in the pocket and zinged the ball down the field. It was one long touchdown pass after another. Marino and his Miami Dolphins embarrassed the Steelers' defense in a 45–28 victory.

Marino might have been the greatest pure passer in NFL history. He did everything just right, from his footwork to his throwing motion. He wasn't a mobile quarterback. But he didn't have to be. His strong, accurate arm and quick decision-making ability made him a force in the pocket.

Dan Marino made history with his powerful passing arm while with the Miami Dolphins in the 1980s and 1990s.

Marino joined the Dolphins in 1983.

His greatest season was 1984. The league MVP shredded defenses as no quarterback had ever done before. His record of 5,084 passing yards stood for 27 years. Marino carried the Dolphins to that season's Super Bowl.

"[It was] a better season than anyone who has ever played this game," said Hall of Fame quarterback Roger Staubach. "I'm talking about quarterbacks, wide receivers, or anyone else. He was unbelievable."

The Dolphins lost Super Bowl XIX to the San Francisco 49ers. It was the only Super Bowl appearance of Marino's 17-year career. He went on to lead the league in passing completions and yards five times. But the Dolphins struggled to build a winning team around him. When Marino retired in 1999, he was the NFL's all-time leader in passing yards (61,361) and passing touchdowns (420).

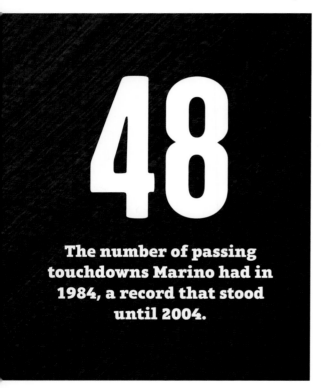

48

The number of passing touchdowns Marino had in 1984, a record that stood until 2004.

Dan Marino calls signals before his Miami Dolphins start a play against the Jacksonville Jaguars in his final season.

DAN MARINO

Hometown: Pittsburgh, Pennsylvania

College: University of Pittsburgh

Height, Weight: 6-foot-4, 224 pounds

Birth Date: September 15, 1961

Team: Miami Dolphins (1983–99)

All-Pro: 1984, 1985, 1986

Pro Bowls: 1983, 1984, 1985, 1986, 1987, 1991, 1992, 1994, 1995

Super Bowl: XIX

JOHN ELWAY

John Elway and the Denver Broncos had the ball at their own 2-yard line.

They trailed the Cleveland Browns 20–13. Only five minutes remained in the conference title game. That's when Elway took charge.

He completed one short pass after the next. When he couldn't find a receiver, he put his head down and ran. With 37 seconds left, he capped off the drive with a touchdown pass. The Broncos had gone 98 yards to tie the game in what became known as "The Drive." Then in overtime, Elway did it again. He threw two long passes and led Denver to the winning field goal. The Broncos were headed to Super Bowl XXI.

Elway had it all. He was big and strong. He had a cannon for an arm. And he knew how to put his team on his shoulders in crunch time.

John Elway came close to championships but always fell short early in his career with the Denver Broncos.

"Great quarterbacks make great plays in great games," he explained. "That's what it's all about, isn't it?" Elway was the face of the Broncos from 1983 to 1998. He led Denver to five Super Bowls and two titles. His best individual season came in 1993. That year he led the league in passing yards and completions.

Elway and the Broncos went to three Super Bowls early in his career. But they lost all three. Elway, however, ended his career by winning two consecutive Super Bowls. He retired at the top of his game. His 51,475 passing yards ranked fourth all-time through 2012. And his 35 career fourth-quarter comebacks ranked third most in league history.

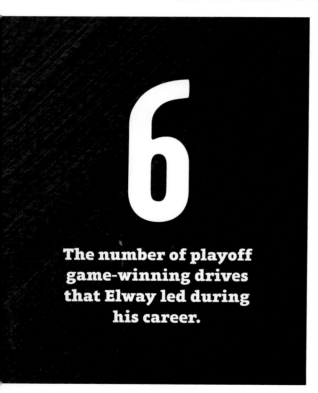

6

The number of playoff game-winning drives that Elway led during his career.

After retiring as a player, Elway worked in the Broncos' front office.

John Elway of the Denver Broncos scrambles during a 1984 win against the New England Patriots.

JOHN ELWAY

Hometown: Port Angeles, Washington

College: Stanford University

Height, Weight: 6-foot-3, 215 pounds

Birth Date: June 28, 1960

Team: Denver Broncos (1983–98)

Pro Bowls: 1986, 1987, 1989, 1991, 1993, 1994, 1996, 1997, 1998

Super Bowls: XXI, XXII, XXIV, XXXII, XXXIII

STEVE YOUNG

Steve Young faced an almost impossible task. He joined the San Francisco 49ers in 1987. And he had to stand and watch on the sidelines as Joe Montana led the team to its third and fourth Super Bowl titles of the 1980s. Then in 1991, Young was tasked with replacing Montana.

It was worth the wait. Young led the NFL in passer rating every year from 1991 to 1994. His best season was 1994. His passer rating of 112.8 was an NFL record. Young was also the league MVP that season, and he led the 49ers to a Super Bowl title. He threw an astonishing six touchdown passes in the 49–26 win over the San Diego Chargers.

Steve Young took over for Joe Montana as the San Francisco 49ers' starting quarterback in 1991.

Young's rise to stardom took longer than most. His first two pro seasons came in the United States Football League (USFL). When that league folded, he joined the NFL's woeful Tampa Bay Buccaneers. Then he had to sit behind Montana for four seasons when he was traded to San Francisco.

112.8

Young's passer rating in 1994. At the time it was an NFL record.

Young became the ultimate dual-threat quarterback. He had one of the most accurate arms in NFL history. His career passer rating of 96.8 ranked him second all-time through 2012. But Young was just as dangerous running the ball. During his career, he ran for 4,239 yards and 43 touchdowns. That made him a nightmare for opposing defenses. They never knew when No. 8 might take off and run for a first down. Young retired after the 1998 season as a two-time league MVP and a seven-time Pro Bowl player.

Steve Young looks to make a play for his San Francisco 49ers against the Dallas Cowboys in 1997.

STEVE YOUNG

Hometown: Salt Lake City, Utah

College: Brigham Young University

Height, Weight: 6-foot-2, 215 pounds

Birth Date: October 11, 1961

Teams: Tampa Bay Buccaneers (1985–86)
San Francisco 49ers (1987–99)

All-Pro: 1992, 1993, 1994

Pro Bowls: 1992, 1993, 1994, 1995, 1996, 1997, 1998

Super Bowls: XXIV, XXIX

WARREN MOON

Houston Oilers quarterback Warren Moon took the snap. He dropped back, scanned the field, and spotted an open receiver. He rifled a 29-yard pass to the end zone for a touchdown. It was Moon's first playoff game, and he led the Oilers to victory.

Moon had a unique football career. He became a pro in 1978. But at the time, the NFL had few black quarterbacks. Many NFL experts didn't think Moon's style was suited to the league. So he instead went to the Canadian Football League (CFL). He was the Edmonton Eskimos' backup for two seasons. Then he became the starter and led the team to three championships in a row.

The Houston Oilers gave Warren Moon a chance after he led the Edmonton Eskimos to three CFL titles.

Moon finally came to the NFL in 1984. Over 17 seasons, he played for the Oilers and three other teams. Moon had a cannon for an arm. He used it to pass for 49,325 yards in his career. That was still the fifth highest total in NFL history through 2012, and it didn't even count the six years he spent in the CFL. Moon led the NFL in passing yards twice and was named Offensive Player of the Year in 1990. He never reached a Super Bowl. But his success helped open doors for future black quarterbacks, such as Donovan McNabb, Cam Newton, and Robert Griffin III.

"[Former Washington Redskins quarterback] Doug Williams and Warren Moon changed the landscape of the National Football League," said former NFL safety Deron Cherry. "They eliminated the myth you couldn't be black and be a quarterback in the NFL."

70,553

The total number of combined passing yards Moon had in the CFL and NFL, a professional record at the time he retired.

Warren Moon of the Houston Oilers tries to make a play while pressured by a Cincinnati Bengals defender in 1990.

WARREN MOON

Hometown: Los Angeles, California

College: University of Washington

Height, Weight: 6-foot-3, 218 pounds

Birth Date: November 18, 1956

Teams: Houston Oilers (1984–93)
Minnesota Vikings (1994–96)
Seattle Seahawks (1997–98)
Kansas City Chiefs (1999–2000)

Pro Bowls: 1988, 1989, 1990, 1991, 1992, 1993, 1994, 1995, 1997

BRETT FAVRE

The Green Bay Packers trailed the New England Patriots in Super Bowl XXXI. Green Bay quarterback Brett Favre took the snap at his own 19-yard line. Favre dropped back and scanned the field. He saw receiver Antonio Freeman break free along the sideline.

Favre let the ball fly. Freeman hauled it in and darted 81 yards to the end zone for a touchdown. It was the longest pass play in Super Bowl history. The Packers took the lead and went on to win the game.

Many great quarterbacks are cool and calculated. Not Brett Favre. He was a true gunslinger. He would throw the ball into the tightest of coverage. It didn't matter if his feet were set or whether he was falling down. Favre always was looking to make a big play.

Brett Favre celebrates a Green Bay Packers touchdown during a playoff game in 2008.

That is why he's the NFL's all-time leader in passing yards, passing touchdowns, completions— and interceptions.

Favre came into the league with the Atlanta Falcons in 1991. But it was one year later, after being traded to the Packers, that he made his mark. After taking over as starting quarterback, he never missed a start in 16 seasons with the Packers. He was the league MVP in 1995, 1996, and 1997. Yet his greatest individual season might have come in 2009 with the Minnesota Vikings. At age 40, Favre posted career bests in completion percentage (68.4 percent) and passer rating (107.2).

Favre retired after the 2010 season. His 71,838 career passing yards were by far the most in NFL history.

321

The number of consecutive regular season and playoff starts Favre made from 1992 to 2010, an NFL record.

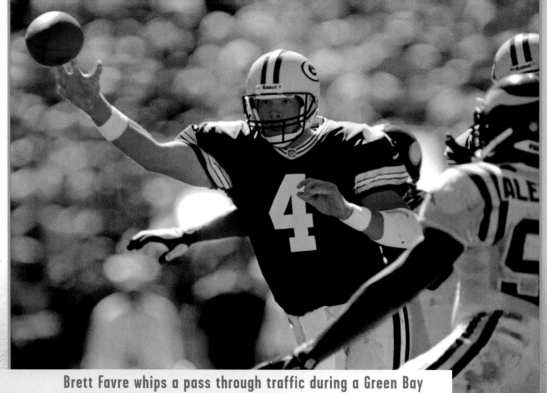

Brett Favre whips a pass through traffic during a Green Bay Packers win over the Minnesota Vikings in 1997.

BRETT FAVRE

Hometown: Kiln, Mississippi

College: University of Southern Mississippi

Height, Weight: 6-foot-2, 225 pounds

Birth Date: October 10, 1969

Teams: Atlanta Falcons (1991)
   Green Bay Packers (1992–2007)
   New York Jets (2008)
   Minnesota Vikings (2009–10)

All-Pro: 1995, 1996, 1997

Pro Bowls: 1992, 1993, 1995, 1996, 1997, 2001, 2002, 2003, 2007, 2008, 2009

Super Bowls: XXXI, XXXII

PEYTON MANNING

Peyton Manning stood behind his offensive line during Super Bowl XLI.
He scanned the field to see what the defense was planning. Spotting a weakness, Manning frantically pointed and barked out signals to his receivers. It's called an audible. Manning took the snap and zipped a pass over the middle of the field. It was caught for a first down.

Manning has always been a student of the game. His dad, Archie, was a successful NFL quarterback, as is his brother, Eli. Peyton Manning has been around pro football most of his life, and it shows. Few quarterbacks have ever had a better feel for the game. Manning controls his offense almost like a coach on the field. Combine that with his strong, accurate arm, and you get one heck of a quarterback.

Peyton Manning was known for calling plays at the offensive line for the Indianapolis Colts.

Manning entered the NFL with the Indianapolis Colts in 1998. For the next 13 seasons, he started in every game the Colts played. During that time, he won four MVP Awards and led the Colts to a Super Bowl title.

All of that changed in 2011. Manning suffered a neck injury and had to miss the entire season. After the season, the Colts released Manning. He signed with the Denver Broncos. Manning proved that he still had it, though. In 2012, he led the Broncos to the best record in the American Football Conference (AFC). He also won the Comeback Player of the Year Award. Even at age 36, Manning proved that he was still one of the best who ever played the game.

4

The number of times Manning has been named league MVP through 2012, an NFL record.

Peyton Manning throws a pass for his Indianapolis Colts during a 2006 game against the Jacksonville Jaguars.

PEYTON MANNING

Hometown: New Orleans, Louisiana

College: University of Tennessee

Height, Wight: 6-foot-5, 230 pounds

Birth Date: March 24, 1976

Teams: Indianapolis Colts (1998–2010)
Denver Broncos (2012–)

All-Pro: 2003, 2004, 2005, 2008, 2009, 2012

Pro Bowls: 1999, 2000, 2002, 2003, 2004, 2005, 2006, 2007, 2008, 2009, 2010, 2012

Super Bowls: XLI, XLIV

TOM BRADY

New England Patriots quarterback Tom Brady took the snap. Receiver Randy Moss streaked down the field. Brady rifled a long pass. Moss rose up and hauled it in for a touchdown. It was Brady's fiftieth touchdown pass of the 2007 season, an NFL record. It also helped the Patriots win the game and complete a perfect 16–0 regular season.

Brady is strong, accurate, and smart. Once he finds a weakness, he attacks. And he's at his best when it matters most. Those qualities have earned him comparisons to his boyhood hero, Joe Montana.

The New England Patriots' Tom Brady looks for an open receiver during Super Bowl XLVI in 2012.

Brady was the 199th player selected in the 2000 NFL Draft. He barely played in his first season. But he got his chance in 2001. He led the Patriots to a Super Bowl victory that season. Then he did it again in 2003 and 2004. His best individual season was 2007. He led the NFL with 4,806 passing yards and 50 touchdown passes. He was named league MVP in 2007 and again in 2010. Through 2012, Brady had 17 career postseason wins as a starting quarterback, the most in NFL history.

17–7

Brady's career playoff record through 2012.

"I really think he might already be the best of all time," Patriots' owner Robert Kraft said. "I watch how involved he is, how driven he is. . . . And he's got a skill that makes him so special, he can process all of it so quickly."

With five Super Bowl appearances, three titles, and a pile of NFL records, Brady may indeed be the greatest to ever play the game.

New England Patriots quarterback Tom Brady throws a pass against the New York Giants in Super Bowl XLII in 2008.

TOM BRADY

Hometown: San Mateo, California

College: University of Michigan

Height, Weight: 6-foot-4, 225 pounds

Birth Date: August 3, 1977

Teams: New England Patriots (2000–)

All-Pro: 2007, 2010

Pro Bowls: 2001, 2004, 2005, 2007, 2009, 2010, 2011, 2012

Super Bowls: XXXVI, XXXVIII, XXXIX, XLII, XLVI

DREW BREES

The New Orleans Saints trailed the Indianapolis Colts by one point late in Super Bowl XLIV. That's when Drew Brees stepped up. Brees led the Saints on a 59-yard touchdown drive. He completed all seven of the passes he threw. And he capped off the drive with a two-yard pass to tight end Jeremy Shockey. The Saints held on and celebrated the team's first championship. Brees raised his one-year-old son over his head as confetti rained down on them.

Nobody throws a better pass than Drew Brees. He has power and accuracy. He can throw a bomb down the field or thread a needle between defenders. His career completion percentage through 2012 was 65.6 percent—third best in league history. And his mark of 71.2 percent in 2011 was the highest ever for a single season.

Drew Brees of the New Orleans Saints showed that shorter quarterbacks could be gunslingers too.

Brees started his career in 2001 with the San Diego Chargers. He was a solid quarterback early on. However, he really became a star after he signed with the Saints in 2006. He led New Orleans to a Super Bowl title after the 2009 season. He also was named Super Bowl MVP. But his 2011 season was even better. Brees threw for a record 5,476 yards. And in 2012, Brees broke Johnny Unitas's record when he threw a touchdown pass in 48 straight games. The streak eventually ended at 54 games.

Brees reached 40,000 passing yards faster than any quarterback in history. If he stays healthy, he might even challenge Brett Favre's NFL-record 71,838 passing yards one day.

3

The number of times Brees had thrown for more than 5,000 yards in a season through 2012. The feat has only been achieved three other times in NFL history.

Drew Brees throws a pass for the New Orleans Saints during a 2007 game against the Tennessee Titans.

DREW BREES

Hometown: Austin, Texas

College: Purdue University

Height: 6-foot, 209 pounds

Birth Date: January 15, 1979

Teams: San Diego Chargers (2001–05)
New Orleans Saints (2006–)

All-Pro: 2006

Pro Bowls: 2004, 2006, 2008, 2009, 2010, 2011, 2012

Super Bowl: XLIV

HONORABLE MENTIONS

Troy Aikman – Aikman ran the potent Dallas Cowboys' offense that won three Super Bowls in the early and mid-1990s.

Sammy Baugh – "Slingin' Sammy" helped change the game during the 1940s, turning it from a league focused almost entirely on running to one that featured downfield passing.

Dan Fouts – Fouts led the NFL in passing yards four straight years from 1979 to 1982 and was a six-time Pro Bowl player with the San Diego Chargers.

Jim Kelly – Kelly was the master of the no-huddle offense that the Buffalo Bills used to win four straight AFC titles in the early 1990s.

Eli Manning – Peyton Manning's little brother secured his place in history by leading the New York Giants to two surprising Super Bowl titles in the 2000s.

Joe Namath – The exciting New York Jets quarterback is best remembered for guaranteeing a win in Super Bowl III, and then delivering in one of the biggest upsets in pro football history.

Aaron Rodgers – Rodgers led the Packers to a Super Bowl title after the 2010 season. Then in 2011, he had the highest quarterback rating (122.5) in league history.

Fran Tarkenton – The Minnesota Vikings' quarterback was an exciting scrambler who, at the time he retired, was the NFL's all-time leader in passing yards (47,003) and touchdowns (342).

Kurt Warner – Despite a late start in his career, Warner led his teams to three Super Bowl appearances and was a two-time league MVP during the late 1990s and early 2000s.

GLOSSARY

audible
A play change called after a team has lined up.

clutch
An ability to perform at one's best in high-pressure situations.

coverage
The placement of defenders against potential receivers; tight coverage means that the defenders are very close to the receivers.

draft
A system used by professional sports leagues to select new players in order to spread incoming talent among teams. The NFL Draft is held each April.

dynasty
A team that wins several titles over a short period of time.

retire
To end one's career.

pump fake
When a passer makes a throwing motion but doesn't let go of the ball in order to fake out defenders.

semipro
A level of sport in which players are paid a very small amount to participate.

West Coast offense
A style of play that focuses on short, safe passes.

FOR MORE INFORMATION

Further Reading

Doeden, Matt. *Tom Brady: Unlikely Champion*. Minneapolis, MN: Twenty-First Century Books, 2011.

Gramling, Gary. *Sports Illustrated Kids 1st and 10: Top 10 Lists of Everything in Football*. New York: Sports Illustrated, 2011.

Kelley, K. C. *Quarterbacks*. Pleasantville, NY: Gareth Stevens Pub., 2010.

Web Sites

To learn more about the NFL's best quarterbacks, visit ABDO Publishing Company online at **www.abdopublishing.com**. Web sites about the NFL's best quarterbacks are featured on our Book Links page. These links are routinely monitored and updated to provide the most current information available.

INDEX

ABOUT THE AUTHOR

Matt Scheff is an author and artist living in Alaska. He enjoys
mountain climbing, fishing, and curling up with his two Siberian
huskies to watch sports.